Sicily

Front cover: The temple of Segesta
Right: The church of San Giovanni, Scicli

TOP 10 ATTRACTIONS

Aeolian Islands. Visit these lovely volcanic islands by hydrofoil. See page 46.

Valley of the Temples. Sicily's most breathtaking ancient site is at Agrigento. See page 70.

Mount Etna. You can take a train around Sicily's smoking volcano. See page 53.

Villa Romana. Many of the finest Roman mosaics ever uncovered are here in Casale. See page 58.